W9-ACB-478

DEATH OF THE KAPOWSIN TAVERN

ALSO BY RICHARD F. HUGO

A Run of Jacks

DEATH OF THE KAPOWSIN TAVERN

RICHARD F. HUGO

Harcourt, Brace & World, Inc.
New York

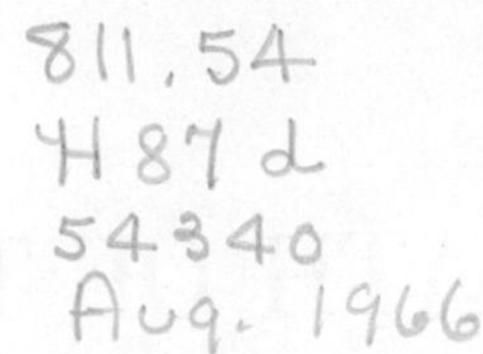

first edition

Library of Congress Catalog Card Number:
65-11990

Printed in the United States of America

Some of the poems in this book appeared in the following magazines: *The Carleton Miscellany, Chrysalis, December, Fresco, Inland, Kayak, Kenyon Review, The Massachusetts Review, The Paris Review, Poetry Northwest, Quarterly Review of Literature, The Sixties,* and *The Yale Review.* "Tahola" and "In Stafford Country" originally appeared in *Poetry*. The poem "Bouquets from Corley" appeared in *Ten Poets, Seattle: 1962.* The following poems also appeared in the anthology *Five Poets of the Pacific Northwest,* University of Washington Press: "Hideout," "Duwamish Head," "Fort Casey, without Guns," and "Graves at Coupeville."

FOR MARTHIEL AND JACKSON MATHEWS

CONTENTS

DUWAMISH, SKAGIT, HOH *1*

Introduction to the Hoh *2*
From the Rain Forest Down *3*
Between the Bridges *5*
Duwamish No. 2 *6*
Bad Vision at the Skagit *7*
Plunking the Skagit *8*
Hideout *10*
Duwamish Head *11*

OTHER WATERS *15*

Tahola *16*
Cape Nothing *17*
Lone Lake, Whidbey *18*
Sweet Piece from Fontal *19*
Dancer at Kozani's *20*
Index *21*
The Anacortes-Sydney Run *22*
Mendocino, Like You Said *23*
The Colors of a Bird *24*
Lake Byron, Maybe Gordon Lord *25*
Road Ends at Tahola *26*

MISSION TO LINZ *27*

LIMITED ACCESS *35*

Eileen *36*
What the Brand New Freeway Won't Go By *37*
December 24 and George McBride Is Dead *38*

Antiques in Ellettsville *39*
The Other Grave *40*
Houses Lie, Believe the Lying Sea *41*
First South and Cambridge *42*
In Stafford Country *43*
For a Northern Woman *44*
Port Townsend *45*
Fort Casey, without Guns *46*
One by Twachtman at the Frye *47*
Bouquets from Corley *48*
The Squatter on Company Land *49*
The Church on Comiaken Hill *50*
The Blond Road *51*
Pike Place Market *52*
Graves at Coupeville *54*
Death of the Kapowsin Tavern *55*

DUWAMISH, SKAGIT, HOH

Introduction to the Hoh

Nearly all the rivers color like the sky
and bend in other places after extra pour.
This blueness is high ice. Cartographers
are smiling at the curves that will recur.

See the white in spring, the milk flow
high enough to run the smaller aspens down.
See there is no urge to lay the sun
across your going like a greasewood patch.

Think of stark abundance, a famous run of jacks
the vanished tribe at the mouth once bragged about.
Think of hungry Mays, the nets reversed
to snag what rot the river washes out.

Glacial melt and tinge are slight in autumn.
Cutthroat backs and pools retain the blue.
Remember famine as these broken leaves
ride away like Indians from you.

From the Rain Forest Down

Click and clatter. Water off for heaven,
loose on bends and bending out of anger
and the fat man groans. Water turns
again and keeps the fat man guessing,
splits the pines and hustles for the open.
Water home to water, free. The fat man
rots all May.

One man was a statue of despair.
Concrete turned the water dirty gray.
A willow grows where an arm should be
and here's the river, shooting for the end,
the statue bobbing by. On the bank
the fat man tips a beer to worldly
river play.

This fat man plays a vicious clarinet
all night, takes food through his eyes,
believes his music makes the current
permanent and warm. He blows a storm—
blows the forest nothing in the rain.
He lives to learn his music only drove
trout upstream.

Now the river slams him with its noise.
His breath comes phony. Worms are crawling
through his clarinet. To the river
he admits he came to stop the flow.
The river laughs his feet away.
The fat man runs to join the marble
in the sea.

Home. The word is dirty. Home is where
the dirty river dies. Dogfish come
to eat the fat from the fat man's eyes.
His clarinet is floating past Marseilles.
In the woods a slender girl decides
to cast herself in stone; for music, whistle
silently.

Between the Bridges

These shacks are tricks. A simple smoke
from wood stoves, hanging half-afraid
to rise, makes poverty in winter real.
Behind unpainted doors, old Greeks
are counting money with their arms.
Different birds collect for crumbs
each winter. The loners don't
but ought to wear red shawls.

Here, a cracked brown hump
of knuckle caved a robber's skull.
That cut fruit is for Slavic booze.
Jars of fruit-spiked bourbon bake
on roofs throughout July; festive tubs
of vegetables get wiser in the sun.
All men are strong. Each woman knows
how river cod can be preserved.

Money is for life. Let the money
pile up thirty years and more.
Not in banks, but here, in shacks
where green is real: the stacks of tens
and twenties and the moss on broken piles
big ships tied to when the river
and the birds ran painted to the sea.

Duwamish No. 2

Mudhens, cormorants and teals take
legal sanctuary in the reeds,
birds and reeds one grey. The river
when the backed-up tide lets go
flows the only north the birds believe.
North is easy. North is never love.

On the west hill, rich with a million
alders and five hundred modern homes,
birds, deep in black, insist the wind
will find the sea. The river points
the wrong way on the in-tide
and the alders lean to the arid south.

Take away all water. Men are oiling
guns beside ripped cows. Wrens have claws
and clouds cascade with poison down
a cliff mapped badly by an Indian.
Tumbleweeds are plotting to stampede.
Where there is no river, pregnant
twice a day with tide, and twice each day
released by a stroking moon,
animals are dangerous as men.

When the world hurts, I come back alone
along the river, certain the salt
of vague eyes makes me ready for the sea.
And the river says: you're not unique—
learn now there is one direction only—
north, and, though terror to believe,
quickly found by river and never love.

Bad Vision at the Skagit

When hills give out, the river loses power.
It started slowing near the State Asylum
and before Mt. Vernon turned into a slough.
Shacks of migrants on the diked bank—
children playing house—male or stark
the wind reminds the farmer and the worker:
soil is rich with men; man ultimately poor.

No lovers love in grass along the shore.
The corn is often stunted. There's some hope
in churches, outlined clean on hills behind
the town. But what design. In stores,
prices climb each payday. The artist
ends up weakly painting buckeye cows.

Mexican and Serb—bending backs and sweat—
European cursing in the grove—wages weak
as yesterday's manure: I should see injustice,
not slow water and the beating birds
that never move a foot against the sun.

Plunking the Skagit

It's mystery, not wind, the men
endure. Steelhead drew them here
where tons of winter drive above
them north and fires start the day
along the bar. A hundred feet
of nylon settles on the river
and the wait begins. Each line slants
tight from an upright rod to water
and underwater to the pencil lead.
A flat south: wind will hammer
water from their eyes, wind and water motion
faking knocks of steelhead in the bells.

These men are never cold. Their faces
burn with winter and their eyes
are hot. They see, across the flat,
the black day coming for them
and the black sea. Good wind
mixes with the bourbon in their bones.

A real name—steelhead—rainbow
from the sea. He runs in summer, too
but that is undramatic, the river
down and warm. No pour to push against.
No ice to snap his fins. No snow
to lay him on for photographs.

Men keep warm with games. The steelhead
is a Burmese spy, a hired gun
from Crete. He comes to mate, not die
on some forgotten sand like salmon.
He rides the river out in spring
planning then his drive for next
December, when big rains bring him
roaring from the sea with fins on fire.

This near the mouth, the river barely glides.
One man thinks the birds that nick
the river mark the fish. Birds believe
the men are evergreens. Above
the guess and ruffle, in the wind—
steelhead to the spawning ground.

Hideout

In the reeds, the search for food by grebes
is brief. Each day, inside the shack
the wind paints white, a man keeps warm
by listening to ships go by, keeps sane
by counting European faces
passing north in clouds. Tugs deposit
miles of logs outside. A tax collector
couldn't find this place with holy maps.

When salmon crowd each other
in the river, and the river boils
with re-creation's anger, what tall man
re-creates too clearly domes of mills
downstream, and the gradual opening
as if the river loved the city
or was crying loudly "take me" to the sea?
What odd games children play.
One shouts himself into a president.
Another pins the villain salmon
to the air with spears. A rowboat
knocks all night against a pile.

Morning brings a new wind and a new
white coat of weather for the shack.
The salmon moved upstream last night
and no bird cuts the river, looking
for a smelt. Ships sail off to Naples
and the bent face bobbing in the wake
was counted in another cloud gone north.

Duwamish Head

1.

That girl upstream was diced by scaling knives—
scattered in the shack I licked her knees in
where she tossed me meat and called me dog
and I would dive a dog at her from stars,
wind around my ears—violins and shot.

With salmon gone and industry moved in
birds don't bite the water. Once this river
brought a cascade color to the sea.
Now the clouds are cod, crossing on the prowl
beneath the dredge that heaps a hundred tons
of crud on barges for the dumping ground.

My vision started at this river mouth,
on a slack tide, trying to catch bullheads
in a hopeless mud. The pier was caving
from the weight of gulls. Wail of tug
and trawl, a town not growing up
across the bay, rotten pay for kings—
these went by me like the secret dawns
the sea brought in. I saw the seaperch
turn and briefly flare around a pile
and disappear. I heard bent men
beg a sole to look less like a stone.

Beyond the squatters and the better homes
stars were good to dive from. Scattered
in the shack I licked her knees in.
Diced, the paper said, by scaling knives.

2.

River, I have loved, loved badly on your bank.
On your out-tide drain I ride toward the sea
so deep the blue cries out in pain from weight.

Loved badly you and years of misery
in shacks along your bank—cruel women
and their nervous children—fishhooks filed
for easy penetration—cod with cracked necks
reaching with their gills for one more day.
Last year's birds are scouting for the kill,
hysterical as always when the smelt run thin.

Jacks don't run. Mills go on polluting
and the river hot with sewage steams.
In bourbon sleep, old men hummed salmon
home to mountains and the river jammed
with blackmouth, boiled in moonlight while the mills
boomed honest sparks. October rolled
with dorsal fins and no man ruled the runs.

When I see a stream, I like to say: exactly.
Where else could it run? Trace it back to ice.
Try to find a photo of your cradle.
Rivers jump their beds and don't look back
regretting they have lost such lovely rides.

I could name those birds, see people
in the clouds. Sight can be polluted
like a river. When this river asks me:
where were you when Slavs gave up their names
to find good homes on paved streets west of here?
I talk back. What are you, river?
Only water, taking any bed you find.
All you have is current, doubled back
on in-tide, screaming out on out.
I am on your bank, blinded and alive.

3.

Where cod and boys had war, a bolt plant roars.
Sparks are stars. Next Sunday, when I die
no drunk will groan my name in spasms
as he vomits last night from the dock.

I have memories of heat upstream.
Her arms and eyes had power like the river
and she imitated salmon with a naked roll.

My vision started at this river mouth
and stuck here (bullhead in the mud)
a third of what could be a lifetime.
The city blares and fishermen are rich.
Tugs and trawls repainted slide to ports
and perch found better color in the sea.

My fins are hands. The river, once
so verbal drifts with such indifference
by me I am forced to shout my name:
backing up on in-tide, screaming out on out—
river, I have loved, loved badly on your bank.

Scattered in the shack I licked her knees in—
beyond her, nothing, just the Indian
I use so often infantile in dreams
of easy winters, five-day runs of silvers,
festive bakes, the passing of the jacks
to sand pools promised by the rain.

To know is to be alien to rivers.
This river helped me play an easy role—
to be alone, to drink, to fail.
The world goes on with money. A tough cat
dove here from a shingle mill on meat
that glittered as it swam. The mill is gone.
The cat is ground. If I say love
was here, along the river, show me bones
of cod, scales and blood, faces in the clouds
so thick they jam the sky with laughter.

OTHER WATERS

Tahola

Where sea breaks inland, claiming the Quinalt
in a half saltwater lake, canoes turn gray
waiting for the runs. The store makes money
but the two cafés, not open, rot in spray.
Baskets you can buy are rumored Cherokee.
When kings run wild, girls use salmon oil
to stain a doll's face real. The best house
was never envied for its tile. Cars
and philosophic eyes are coated by the sea.

Whites pay well to motor up the river,
harvest blackmouth, humpbacks, silvers,
jacks and sea run cuts. Where rain assaults
the virgin timber and the fishpools boil,
the whites pry stories from the guide
with bourbon. Sunset, and they putt downriver
singing. But the wind, the sea
make all music language, dead as a wet drum.

When whites drive off and the money's gone
a hundred mongrels bark. Indians
should mend the tribal nets in moonlight,
not drink more and hum a white man's tune
they heard upstream. What about the words?
Something about war, translated by the sea
and wind into a song a doll sang
long ago, riding a crude wave in.

Cape Nothing

The sea designed these cliffs. Stone is cut
away odd places like a joke.
A suicide took aim, then flew out
in the arc he thought would find the sea.
He came down hearing "sucker" in the wind,
heard it break at "suck-" and all the time
tide was planning to ignore his bones.

Far out, the first white roll begins.
What an easy journey to this shore,
gliding miles of water over stars
and mudshark bones that laugh through tons
of green. You can time that wave and wind
by tripling your memory of oars.
The sea will con the gold from our remains.

Foam is white. When not, no dirtier
than bones gone brown with waiting for the sea.
When wind deposits spray on bone
bone begins to trickle down the sand.
Now the bones are gone, another shark
abandoned to the sea's refractive lie.
The moon takes credit for the boneless rock.

Bones don't really laugh beneath the sea.
They yawn and frown through green at time
and lie in squares to kid the moon
and drive stars from the water with the gleam
of phosphorus gone mad. Now a diver
poses on the cliff for passing cars
before he flies out singing "water, I am yours"

Lone Lake, Whidbey

(FOR DAVE WAGONER)

The sun, the warm man renting boats
and warm farms slanting to the lake
decide the wind is warm. Our numb
hands fight the anchor rope. We drift
to a wobbly stop in lilies.

That green crud (algae) makes this lake
look stagnant every May. Chorus-
girls could strut along that shore
or a king replace the farms he burned
with castles, but the blackbird
on the reed that bows defeated
will remain, his red ignited
by the wind. A reel is singing nylon
down the guides, and in that second sky
a line is moving, terrified.
Blood and rainbow sides are also red.

Underwater, the farms go on.
Catfish graze like cattle in the weeds
and trout fly over the catfish
like those high birds without form
or name, flying the morning away.

Sweet Piece from Fontal

My darling we are trolling Lake Fontal,
slipping by the snags that jut from moss,
skirting beds of pads. Two trailing spoons
flash a sneaky hunger to the trout.
Guess what monster levels on the gleam—
five pounds in the oven, losing oil
and sizzling with fun, grinning in his heat.
That's a fishhawk frowning from the pine.

We came here on a slow and dirty road.
Now we slide on glass, trusting clouds
to braze the surface, blur the sight of trout.
I wheel the boat and never cross our lines.
Rainbows nick our spoons. Behind the boat
the trout that bends your tip is jumping,
spitting out your hook and going.
That's a fishhawk frowning from the pine.

Other lakes are roasting in those hills.
Their steam will never singe a pine,
cannot bake a fishhawk though we hate him.
Highland lakes so high only condors
find them, rage alive with rainbow
fatter than a day with thirty days.
That's a fishhawk frowning from the pine.

That's a fishhawk frowning from the pine.
Let him frown. That crank can't fly or drink
or know what trouble drove us to this lake.
Clouds are years gone north and wind is playing
light about your face. Let's troll until
we take a double creel, then row for home,
our hunger pounding and our fishing rods broke down.

Dancer at Kozani's

Through the white chiffon that covered her
we whipped her with our eyes until
she crawled the floor in heat.
When she got up, disrobed and shook
the wall got wet. The lute
that led her shimmy stung her thighs.

Swish of red hair on the floor, twitch
of buttock, breast line clean in shake—
she danced us into war and back
and when the fiddle tied her to a rock
she wiggled free. Her legs were wild
as pillars to a Persian lost in wind.
When far strings tore her from our sight
what vain trout circled in our wine?

We swam out into the smothering night
praying for rain to wash the smoke away.

Index

The sun is caked on vertical tan stone
where eagles blink and sweat above
the night begun already in the town.
The river's startling forks, the gong
that drives the evening through the pass
remind the saint who rings the local chime
he will be olive sometime like a slave.

Screams implied by eyes of winded eagles
and wind are searing future in the stone.
The cliff peels off in years of preaching water
and the cliff remains. The saint is red
to know how many teeth are in the foam,
the latent fame of either river bed
where trout are betting that the saint is brown.

Flakes of eagle eggshells bomb the chapel
and the village ears of sanctuary dumb.
In a steaming room, behind a stack
of sandbagged books, the saint retreats
where idols catch a fever from his frown.
The saint is counting clicks of eagle love.
The river jumps to nail a meaty wren.

And April girls enlarge through layers
of snow water, twitching fish and weeds
and memories of afternoons with gills.
If a real saint says that he could never
see a fiend, tell that saint to be here,
throat in hand, any Friday noon—
delirious eagles breed to tease the river.

The Anacortes-Sydney Run

In my best dream I have crossed the border
and my coins are wrong. Without the tongue
I gesture, sweat and wake aboard this boat.
Ladies in their staterooms write bad poems—
mountains in the distance evidence of God.
Maps are hard to read. Two nations own
these islands. The shade of green on one
could be Canadian, but firs and grebes
are mine. The latest run of Springs
are far too international to claim.
Yet they use our rivers for their graves.

The law protects the San Juans. No bilge here.
Gulls still trail the ferry but go hungry.
You can buy an island. In my worst dream
I am living here, contented and alone.
That house is mine. The blue smoke rising
means I'm cooking. Constant knock of water
means I'm drunk, enjoying private jokes
and bowing as the walls begin to roar.
The Coast Guard breezes by my door.
They haven't stopped to chat in twenty years.

In no dream I am standing on this deck
admiring the sheep on what turns out
to be the final island before landing.
I woke up dead among these islands—
this boat chugging in a bad direction—
the north I go, my wake already fading.

Mendocino, Like You Said

(FOR ROBERT PETERSON)

From China contra-boom-bang water
jars the cliffs, spray above the roofs
of homes on stilts. Boats and hotel rot.
Russians doubt a profit from the road
or sea. Water cracking fathoms
into sky, the grass that moves by green alone
when wind is gone, say be alive.

We say die. We say catch the world
without the neon, only iron, wood
and clay and dated. See how the sad
is best reflected in a face when albacore
are weighed. Despite old poems and songs,
women on the shore are far too tough
to be there simply waiting for the men.
The boats are in but no one plans a dance.
No two talk an hour after anchor.

The sea's a band. A far-off clarinet
is coming on. The ocean blows the grass.
Birds are driven landward close enough
to claim. We know we're weak and wrong
but music and another knee
refill our eyes with a keen butane.

The Colors of a Bird

A bird sails from the hole in that high stone,
circles once and glides down, humming
with his wings. He seemed white half-
way up, but green now as he ticks
the river. No one doubts the water.
It will eat the best men from the sky.

Gold. Not gold, but blue. The tan bird
in and out of sunlight hugs the stream.
Now he uses cedar bark for amber,
takes the color of a hostile man.
He has no taste. How satisfied he seems
anywhere he flies throughout the spectrum.

He found shades of pink in Italy.
Man can give one color only,
promise birds a perfect afternoon:
trout and worm, a coy girl brought to answer
in the grass. The bird will never brown
hoping for the sun this river flicks.

The red bird sweeps the evening water flat.
Picnics never work. The army
separates in current as they drown.
Now the laughing black bird draws
a hectic line of nothing on the air
and drives relieved into the rocky dark.

Lake Byron, Maybe Gordon Lord

(FOR PATT WAGONER)

Deep in that black water where you tossed a book
of Byron, trout have read Don Juan
and are fighting mad. Madness like the mushroom
pushing rocks aside to rise is latent
in your past. Despite the wealthy cabins,
owls you spot are right for disapproving.
You are right for loving birds with scowls.

Only wars without a name have meaning.
Byron died for nothing. What rare hawk
reduces you to meat with perfect circles?
How easily you draw him as a woman—
coy lids fallen, head half turned away—
"You can't mean me." You know the problem.
How to earn a talon. You earn yourself
by showing birds a way to be afraid.

I'm no stranger to the darker waters.
True, they half disown me, but the stars
are bound to stutter when the crappie ripe
with gold assemble and you paint them.
Not really well, but saying fish are birds
and birds are stars and keep your head down.
Don't think too much when young about the heavens.

Byron must be rotting in the mud.
I don't know what water does to paper,
but it must be awful, like one human
to another. You're a hawk's authority
on what it takes to die and then recover.

Road Ends at Tahola

My nostrils tell me: somewhere *mare nostro.*
Here the wolf-fish hides his lumpy face in shame.
Pines lean east and groan. Odors of a booze
that's contraband, are smuggled in by storms.
Our booze is legal Irish and our eyes
develop felons in the endless spray.
Mare nostro somewhere, and eternity's
a law, not a felony like here.
That derelict was left for storms to break.

One ship passes denting the horizon,
creeping down the world. Whatever gave us pride
(food en route to Rio) dies. The wake could be
that wave we outrun laughing up the sand.
Night comes on with stars and years of dead fish
lighting foam with phosphorus they left.
All day the boom was protest, sea against
the moon. *Mare nostro* somewhere and no shame.

Remember once, a scene, a woman naked
clowning in the sea while armies laughed.
Her man, a clown, had courage and he came
and hauled her (both were sobbing) up the stones.
If I were strong, if wolf-fish didn't dive
beyond the range of scorn, you'd be alive.

I can't say *mare nostro.* Groaning pines
won't harm you, leaning east on galaxies.
I know I'm stone. My voice is ugly.
A kelp bed is a rotten place to hide.
Listen. Hear the booming. See the gleam,
the stars that once were fish and died.
We kiss between the fire and the ocean.
In the morning we will start another stare
across the gray. Nowhere *mare nostro.*
Don't claim it and the sea belongs to you.

MISSION TO LINZ

1

If you look at the sky
north, there where it ends
as if finite or breaks its northern orange,
in a vacuum of time
you might suddenly know this:
that the sky where it ends does not end
and you will pass its horizons.

You must know it before
you can think of it, speak of it;
it must come on you more sudden than flare
before you identify yourself with the power:
the olive with yellow band death in the bay,
the Pratts, the Hamilton Standards,
the Norden, turrets of fifty calibers.

It must seem weird, incommunicable
the desire for ozone
cold and the unremembered terrible.

You could realize an angel in orange
between the Alps, blue in summer, and the spray of cirrus
but that is visual and will not do
and besides it is remembered beautiful.

Or you might hear the rotation to come,
the thunder of revolving iron,
the padded burst blackening under the nose,
sound of the almighty sickening
but that is auditory and will not do
and besides it is remembered terrible.

You can see the gunners smoking
on the morning stones.
The navigator tugging his harness.
The pilot who checks everything twice.

The good-natured bombardier
or co-pilot swearing.
They too could look at the sky
north, there where it ends
as if finite or breaks its northern orange,
and in that moment of no time know it:
where they will be in hours
of rotation and revolving iron
before they can think of it,
speak of it.

It must seem weird, incommunicable
the desire for ozone
cold and the unremembered terrible.

You can know it.
It will come on you quickly.
But even if you can say it,
once the engines have started nothing is heard.

2

Nothing is heard in the north,
and the northern temperatures grow cold with the height.
There is the stark crack of voice
taking oxygen checks and the sharp static answers.
You are beyond birds, a season called summer.
There are places away from the world where the air is always
winter.
Nothing is heard in the north.

The engines pound out their particular fever
a sound that has a silence of its own.
There is the control of needles and gauges, green
and showing the speed, the degrees and the climb,
and the six boxes of six shudder and rock
where the sun goes pale in the thinness of air
above the Adriatic. Fifties are tested,

checked in
with the stark crack of six voices
and the seventh replying with a sharp static answer.
And the engines pound out their particular fever
a sound that has a silence of its own.

No one can call this movement
though Europe wavers and falls back to the south
and a needle says one-fifty-four. The air
is ten centuries of waiting. A flange
is your breathing and the throat says nothing
behind the tight mask, and the mask,
the silent engines are all your loss of self.

The sterile Alps, blue in summer
swing up, pass for an hour underneath,
fall harshly into their brown valleys
and the grey one rail towns of vertical protection.

But what do you think
while Europe wavers and falls back to the south
in a way that is not called movement?
While the flange breathes for you
and the needles swing to other numbers?

Europe wavers and falls back to the south,
the silence rotates your life in the roar
and you think this:
that out of thirty-six we stand a chance
(statistic) to lose three at the most.
Twenty minutes before the wide turn
you will say it over and over
where the air is twenty centuries of tension
and the sun goes pale in the thinness of air
you will say it: three at the most.

But the engines pound out their particular fever.
A silence of its own.
There are places away from the world where the air is always
winter.
Nothing is heard in the north.

3

You fly north to a point, swing slowly
to the east, open your belly and brace
before the eight-minute course, planned
on violet maps a smile before, but now
Linz opens like a flower below your nose
and the silence drives louder airs into the bay.
The dagger black explodes and the praying increases
until the over-ripe melon of day, cracking its hide
shows the red-moist fear just back of your brows.

A plane evaporates so quickly,
silently, it might have been
from magic were it not your fear
knew ten reduced molecular.
There is the silence and the waiting
in eight-minute vacuum, and black puffing
thick as enormous dark rain,
some, the close, sounding, a few
the very close, jolting.

Out of the thirty-five still airborne
there was a moment, one
your dreams will lose, stopped in tiny fire,
flipped dizzily away,
a wing peeled back like a sudden unloosening arm
fluttered down five miles of sky as paper,
and you didn't hear a thing.

And the moment
when the sky split open, allowed
the lazy tons of yellow-banded children
to fall in forty-second wonder, converge
in a giant funnel. Now you
who, so high, can only see
the puff like a penny dropped in dust
at your toe on a country road, rack up
and out, down with a speed
that strains the blueprint—until
noiselessness, the level back
into clean sky.

Of all this, this, and only it:
you can forget, and will, the degrading prayer
when the sound is gone, only this:
you feel good to your own touch,
you remain.

4

Summer is heard in the south,
and the southern temperatures grow warm as you drop.
The speed is easier, the brain
warmed by the sound of insult,
and you defend yourself by making fun
of others' fear, of your own prayers.
You come into birds, a sun that is warmer.
There is land away from the sky where the sound is always
summer.

There is the needle control, the green gauges
showing the speed, the degrees and the fall.
The engines sing you to the home of men,
the earth, and think of it; its brownness,
its solidity, its greenness. You can build
warm rooms on its hills, love on it,
and if you die on it you remain
long enough to be lied about, buried in it.

Anyone can call this movement.
Europe speeds back to the north. The Adriatic
glimmers its blues to the brown shores of summer
and the engines sing you to the home of men,
the earth, and think of it.

If you think of it you know soil
is its own loveliness and you want to be on it
to drink, speak and study friends' faces.

If you think about it for a long time
the mind, like engines, will sing
you to the home of men,
where concerts carry
fast in summer wind.

LIMITED ACCESS

Eileen

Why this day you're going so much [illegible]
When you've gone, I'll go back in alone
and take the stillest corner in the house—
the [illegible]
will find me whipped and choking back my [illegible].
I won't show my hatred to their food.
I have to live here with these shaking hands.

Find a home with heat, some stranger
who's indifferent to your dirty dress
and loves you for that quiet frown
you'll wear until you die or kiss.
The wind is drowning out the car
and raising dust so you can disappear
the way you used to playing in the [illegible].

Someday I'll be too big for them to hit,
too fast to catch, too quick to face the cross
and go away by fantasy or mile
and take revenge on [illegible] for your [illegible]
and mail you word of faces I have cut,
be patient when the teasers call you [illegible].
I'll [illegible] later for [illegible].

Then I'll stroke the [illegible] from your hair.
The [illegible] me now [illegible] here.
I was their [illegible], [illegible]
they wait and wait for dust to settle
on the road you left on centuries ago,
believing you were waving, knowing
it was just a bird who crossed the road
behind you and the sunlight off the car.

Eileen

Why this day you're going so much wind?
When you've gone I'll go back in alone
and take the stillest corner in the house—
the dark one where your dark-eyed ghost
will find me whipped and choking back my rage.
I won't show my hatred to their food.
I have to live here with these shaking hands.

Find a home with heat, some stranger
who's indifferent to your dirty dress
and loves you for that quiet frown
you'll own until you die or kiss.
The wind is drowning out the car
and raising dust so you can disappear
the way you used to playing in the fern.

Some day I'll be too big for them to hit,
too fast to catch, too quick to face the cross
and go away by fantasy or mule
and take revenge on matrons for your loss
and mail you word of faces I have cut.
Be patient when the teasers call you fat.
I'll join you later for a wordless meal.

Then I'll stroke the maggots from your hair.
They come for me now you're not here.
I wax their statues, croak out hymns
they want and wait for dust to settle
on the road you left on centuries ago,
believing you were waving, knowing
it was just a bird who crossed the road
behind you and the sunlight off the car.

What the Brand New Freeway Won't Go By

The block is bare except for this five-story
ugly brick hotel. Perhaps the bulk
frightened stores and homes away. Age is clear
in turrets and the milk on window sills.
The new name and the outside coat of paint
must have raised the rent. As you drive by
the rooms seem yellow and the air inside
is stale because a roomer, second floor,
in underwear, unshaven, fries a meal.

To live here you should be a friend of rain,
and fifty with a bad job on the freights,
knowing the freeway soon will siphon
the remaining world away
and you can die unseen among your photos—
swimmers laughing but the day remembered cold.

Rooms have gas. The place was in the papers.
Police have issued statements about cancer
and the case is closed, but not the jokes
passing boys are drilling through the walls.
Top-floor renters look down floors of sweat
to traffic that might stop were they to go.
Some rooms are paid for in advance with shock.

If, when the freeway opens, a man
afraid of speed still takes this road,
the faded Under New Management sign
might mean to him: we are older too—
live here—we'll never treat you badly again.

December 24 and George McBride Is Dead

You a gentleman and I up from the grime—
now wind has shut your dark, dark eyes
and I am left to hate this Christmas eve.
Christ, they're playing carols. Some crap
never stops. You're dead and I'm without
one goddam Wagner record in the house
to play you up to what for some must be
behind the sky with solid orchestration.

Rest in your defeat, you stupid jerk,
so fat your heart gave out, so sweet
you couldn't help but hear the punks.
"One gulp. The whole quart, Mac." That town
you died in—so unlikely—vineyards,
sunny valleys, stark white missions
and the pale priest summoning
brown sinners from the olive grove.
I'll not know your grave, though I believe
our minds have music that can lead us
through the tangle to the lost stone of a friend.

I get along, write my poems. Essentially
a phony, I try my feelings now
and know I fail. George, it's Christmas eve
and bells are caroling. I'm in the kitchen,
fat and writing, drinking beer and shaking.

Antiques in Ellettsville

(FOR ANN MC GARRELL)

That nine-foot doughboy, were the sculptor good,
would be at war. What bayonet, what snarl
can win against the shade of pleasant oaks,
the road that makes an open store seem closed?
On that plate, a rose survives the cracks.
Faces crack with age. The owner
leaves her beans to brag about the pewter.
Miss Liberty is steadfast in an oval frame.

Fun to laugh the past away—silly words
etched lovingly in gold—eyes so tough
and ignorant the photograph went gray—
a farm that might still be—a Clydesdale team.
Now we trade-in chrome to hide the wear
or hide behind next year, afraid of Hoosiers
waving old hellos from older porches.

Our problem is the value of the old,
the value of the cruel. A sadist thinks
a bruise is just a rose. Pyromaniacs
would bruise this town to cinder
had they not gone big-time in the east. Out west
the oldest thing is neon. Here, the antiques
warn us to be tolerant of dust.

Let's run and love the old and know tomorrow
whatever trails our running leave in air
a tiny crone will price and call antique.
Why not a giant soldier for your lawn—
his bayonet as level as your frown
when salesmen come, their baskets heavy
with those bullets armies wouldn't buy.

The Other Grave

Long and smelling good, the cemetery grass
could be a kiss. You failed a field
of Ypsilanti wheat. Below your stone
you never try to touch her there beside you.
I used to blame your failure on the moon.

When old, you needed words like "lake."
"Lake" I'd say. Your eyes began to farm.
Horses took you and a friend where coves
were wonderful with bass—bluegills
clowning for your rind below the log.
Catfish ran five pounds. See my picture.
See my mustache then. Any photo fades.
You remain in yellow with your catch.

I'd like to sing you, point each word
about you up and shoot. Wasn't gold
too easy for your maps, or love
too simple for your brilliant arms?
I said a British wind was in your face—
only blue the undertaker planned.
The tunes you hummed were so unknown
I told a dog you were a fine composer.

Why am I afraid or sorry you are dead?
My hands paid contraband to be this still.
My mouth rotted with the truth
to be as tough as wheat before your stone.

Houses Lie, Believe the Lying Sea

Forget the keep-off sign. That cow
is no detective paid to guard this house
and the barricade is rot. Inside
the stove is moldy. Sunlight rays
through slits to spot the dust we breathe.
Rooms are sick for light. That male doll
fractured in the corner means
the rage of children went remote
in sea light and the humming flies.

The well still works. Pump, and water
coughs out brown. Did a father weep
and shout at weeping children: we are poor?
And when they moved without a buyer,
did the mother turn Chinese with shame?
An empty house can teach a rat despair.

Decay is often moss, green when grass
is dirty, tan or dying. Someone's due
to tend the cow. The meadows slant
a way they didn't when we entered.
Those rooms will be remembered vaguely
years from now in Greece. Who's for loving
on those rags, that broken glass?
Let's go loving where the ocean
scatters on the rocks to die like homes.

First South and Cambridge

Sandbanks climb and curve until
a stadium. Brief bones gleam
in grey-brown bars of periods
that end in -cene. Say monster
and the wind roars animate
about the walls. A sparrow pecks
at 70 A.D. The jaw you dig
is just a dog, no scientific coup.

The banks have Indian voices
or turn Sicilian in the heat
or promise over the top, green
hills spread out for lovers
and a brook no man has seen.
But there, salal, though green
is far too stiff for romance
and Hitler left his rubbers in the creek.

When sand is covered over (alders
grow in sand) you might hope
for another end—banks exploding,
robins caught in tiny slides, each
grain a boulder Indians roll down.
But these banks, once so urgent
in their Sunday need-to-be
pace their end a little slower
than you fight the end of sand.

In Stafford Country

No hills. Raw wind unchecked, brings word
of death from Texas. No shade. Sun bruises
the oats gold. With homes exposed
no wonder people love. Farms absorb
the quiet of the snow, and birds
are black and nameless miles away.

Without a shield of hills, a barricade
of elms, one resorts to magic, hiding
the joker well behind the gesturing hand.
Childish wars continue in our minds.
Paint is the gray it was in Carthage.

Where land is flat, words are far apart.
Each word is seen, coming from far off,
a calm storm, almost familiar, across
the plain. The word floats by, alive.
Homes are empty and the love goes on
as the odor of grain jumps in the wind.

For a Northern Woman

I reach for you. You smile and I am male.
Mornings when we stroll this pale canal,
past these poplars factories turned brown,
yet with height and swing insisting
they are green, your eyes say what north
you're from. They call me man. Your hair
is orphan as I break it in my hand.

Lady, I control you. On command
you kiss some old stream south to home.
Let's name what's warm along this quay:
the trawl that pounds desire for the sea,
pregnant cats, fishing men who need
no fish, the ancient hanging wash.
My plan for you is cruel: to roast you
in the light I steal from your blonde form.

Smile me male again. Or never smile
by this canal gone gray from waste
or from that early sky the northern know.
Poplars stretch so far above us, branches
tick the sun. I know that aching bark.
I ache to cast you hot in northern stone.

Port Townsend

On cliffs above the town, high homes disdain
what is not Victorian below
but Indian or cruel. A plaque declares
a chapel older than the town.
(Many worship God before they're born.)
The Keystone ferry sails without a car,
a passenger, not even trailing gulls.
The pulp mill shoots bad odor at the sun.

Arriving here is feeling some old love—
half a memory—a silly dream of how
a war would end, a world would settle down
with time for hair to gray before you die.
The other half of memory is sight.
The cliffs will hold another thousand years.
The town is rotting every Sunday night.

A novel fakes a start in every bar,
gives way to gin and talk. The talk gives way
to memories of elk, and elk were never here.
Freighters never give this town a second look.
The dead are buried as an afterthought
and when the tide comes glittering with smelt
the grebes have gone to look for meaty ports.

Fort Casey, without Guns

(FOR RAE TUFTS)

The iron doors we shut on ammo rooms
slam like a heart attack. Had the guns remained,
grass would still be busted by July to straw
and riptides groan as current doubles back
in hatred. Concrete walls were hopes
of pioneers, one shade deeper gray each spring.
From these emplacements, ten-inch cannons tracked
fifty years of freighters down the strait.
The sea shot out the gunners' eyes with light.
The army moved to Coupeville in defeat.

What's left to save, the riptide will protect.
We joke our way through battlements,
dim powder huts, the corridors where words explode
and we are skeletons, trapped by a mistake—
the wrong door closed, a turn we didn't make.
We claw at rungs to take us into sky.

Straw bales on the muster ground deny
a need for war. The farmer doesn't care.
The strait can go unguarded, pagan ships
sail in with slave girls and a threat of fun—
the Stars-and-Stripes torn down—the Constitution
used to start a fire for the wienie roast.
Only harvest matters. Here, the army
harvested no enemy. Even boredom cracked—
contraband steamed down in 'twenty-eight—
the bootleg wink—rum for rotting men.

Best to come here when the picnics peter out.
On dark days, gulls are shells (man will not disarm)
and we can play our war. I am a captain.
Make that cloud salute. The Olympics
bomb the strait with shadow. In the meadow
where October green begins, cattle eat
and children point their space guns at us,
crying boom the booming sea can't hear.

One by Twachtman at the Frye

The flags beyond those dunes are roaring.
Carnival here. Freaks for the fun of children.
Taffy and games. Beyond the din, the sea
compounds the joy. Ships go by,
plenty of fuel and no destination.
Beyond the sea, you feel, people are living,
happy and loving, no hymns or diseases.

You cannot cross that sand to the fun.
That friendless grass prohibits what chance
you might have to shake phantoms of lust—
two women fighting over your body,
the loser to love you, the winner to die.
They always fight dirty in dreams.
You always hear the games in the wind.
You are never closer, forever held back by the sand.

Someday you'll cross it, enter the gate
of the gayway, win all the money,
eat yourself sick and come back relaxed
to these dunes, and here find your bones
friendless as grass, covered with laughter
and flags the seawind tore from the poles.

Bouquets from Corley

Are these flowers paint? Back of each bouquet,
behind the eyes of good men, odor beats.
It's not the fault of some damn cow we knew
that our hands go slowly blue from work.
Flowers will be ruined by a storm or painted.
Roses flare in ancient loams of thieves.

That Friday everyone is born on
slides into a weekend for our leisure—
walking streets and sensing Ward's bouquets—
rage in the composure, regret in color
fading back into a childhood weather—
oil diluting rain to save the garden.

In hills where hate began, cows are flowers.
Udders swing and seem remote in gray.
Outside the gallery, roses are composed
by rain and killed. Paint does not wash off.
In painting, roses have the sense to be afraid,
knowing it's not the fault of an old cow
that a flower, like a man, left one weather
for another long ago to live.

The Squatter on Company Land

We had to get him off, the dirty elf—
wild hair and always screaming at his wife
and due to own our land in two more years—
a mud flat point along the river
where we planned our hammer shop.
Him, his thousand rabbits, the lone goat
tied to his bed, his menial wife: all out.

To him, a rainbow trail of oil might mean
a tug upstream, a boom, a chance a log
would break away and float to his lasso.
He'd destroy the owners' mark and bargain
harshly with the mill. He'd weep and yell
when salmon runs went by, rolling
to remind him he would never cheat the sea.

When did life begin? Began with running
from a hatchet some wild woman held,
her hair a gray cry in alfalfa
where he dug and cringed? Began in rain
that cut the light into religious shafts?
Or just began the way all hurt begins—
hit and dropped, the next man always righteous
and the last one climbing with a standard tongue?

In his quick way, swearing at us pressed
against the fence, he gathered rags and wood
and heaped them in the truck and told his wife
"Get in," and rode away, a solid glare
that told us we were dying in his eye.

The Church on Comiaken Hill

(FOR SYDNEY PETTIT)

The lines are keen against today's bad sky
about to rain. We're white and understand
why Indians sold butter for the funds
to build this church. Four hens and a rooster
huddle on the porch. We are dark
and know why no one climbed to pray. The priest
who did his best to imitate a bell
watched the river, full of spirits, coil
below the hill, relentless for the bay.

A church abandoned to the wind is portent.
In high wind, ruins make harsh music.
The priest is tending bar. His dreams have paid
outrageous fees for stone and mortar.
His eyes are empty as a chapel
roofless in a storm. Greek temples seem
the same as forty centuries ago.
If we used one corner for a urinal,
he wouldn't swear we hadn't worshipped here.

The chickens cringe. Rain sprays chaos where
the altar and the stained glass would have gone
had Indians not eaten tribal cows
one hungry fall. Despite the chant,
salmon hadn't come. The first mass
and a phone line cursed the river.
If rain had rhythm, it would not be Latin.

Children do not wave as we drive out.
Like these graves ours may go unmarked.
Can we be satisfied when dead
with daffodils for stones? These Indians—
whatever they once loved or used for God—
the hill—the river—the bay burned by the moon—
they knew that when you die you lose your name.

The Blond Road

This road dips and climbs but never bends.
The line it finally is strings far beyond
my sight, still the color of useless dirt.
Trees are a hundred greens in varying light
as sky breaks black on silver over and in
the sea. Not one home or car. No shacks
abandoned to the storms. On one side,
miles of high grass; on the other, weather
and the sea reflecting tons of a wild day.

The wind is from Malay. Tigers in the wind
make lovers claw each other orange. Blond
dirt rises to recite the lies of summer
before the wind goes north and cats rip
white holes in the sky. Fields are grim
and birds along this road are always stone.

I planned to cheat the road with laughter.
Build a home no storm could crack
and sing my Fridays over centuries of water—
once more, have me back, my awkward weather—
but the land is not for sale. Centuries
are strung: a blond road north and south
and no man will improve it with macadam.

The road is greased by wind. Sun has turned
the blond dirt brown, the brown grass
black and dark ideas of the ocean
silver. Each month rolls along the road
with an hour's effort. Now the lovers
can't recall each other or identify
that roar: the northern pain of tigers.

I know that just a word I'll never have
could make the brown road blond again
and send the stone birds climbing to their names.

Pike Place Market

In many tongues, hawkers scream our fingers
off the fruit display. All day, we never see
the rows of lightbulbs shining. Rages faked
by blinding grapes and pears make eating
cosmopolitan. In *The Athenian*
Negro faces do no better than the white
against the sea outside. A prude might wait
long enough to see the U.S. Fleet pull out.
Voyeurs keep dark islands in reserve.

Behind their eyes, old men are shooting moons
with yellow guns. Solly cleans a carp
with carvings doctors and a thug would envy.
These market skills go back to deep in Egypt,
deep in dynasties of dirt, in minds
of cats who hug the market in a storm.
Here, it is assumed all things have value.
The world will not wear out. Best-selling
paperbacks with covers bruised by grease:
one dime. No bargaining, though produce
can be talked down sharply after five.

Who plans to tear this market down?
Erect a park? Those militants who hate
the old and odd, and dream of homes where lawns
are uniformly green. Who gloats at space for rent,
stalls abandoned, fire that destroyed
those baskets Indians will never weave again
and turned a case of rump roasts into char?

Let the columns rot, progressive mayors deny
a city has a private right to be.
Let the market slide into the sea.
The sea has meat, is derelict and kind.
Snapper, red from failure, live on sun.
No bass ever knew another, and the pompano
like men arranged to be alone.

Market. In November, drink the darkness in
and make the dark your closing. Burlesque
rows of lightbulbs that were lit all day,
shine for the first time, glinting
off a pigeon and the rinsed cement
and women poking in the garbage for a meal.

Graves at Coupeville

When weather shouted at us: vagabond
we looked for weathered towns where men are strange.
Our clothes were older than these stones where words
erased by moss are silly said aloud.
We had idols that the light deranged.
Last night's strangers could have been our friends.
The dead were singing slogans in our blood.

Think of walls your insufficient fist bounced off,
walls your face ran down and couldn't stain
and I was turned away by smiling aides,
couldn't find a job. Why a car so old?
Why the world so new, the men so knowing?
Don't the wounded find a use for mold?
We need no introduction to these plots.

That's the captain—lost his head to knives
of Haidas. That's a smuggler and that
a sentimental fool. Read his epitaph:
Mary. We love one another still.
I'll go first. You mark my stone with lines
the south wind often writes on zany days.
Dump me in a river roaring for the sea.

We joke back across the strait at islands.
Men are islands. Haidas live in carvings
in stockades men turn into museums.
We never give old guns another glance.
Taste your tears, the lime of them, the liquor.
Give the foolish dead a second chance.
The weather hates our poses
but the sun deranges men with laughter.

Death of the Kapowsin Tavern

I can't ridge it back again from char.
Not one board left. Only ash a cat explores
and shattered glass smoked black and strung
about from the explosion I believe
in the reports. The white school up for sale
for years, most homes abandoned to the rocks
of passing boys—the fire, helped by wind
that blew the neon out six years before,
simply ended lots of ending.

A damn shame. Now, when the night chill
of the lake gets in a troller's bones
where can the troller go for bad wine
washed down frantically with beer?
And when wise men are in style again
will one recount the two-mile glide of cranes
from dead pines or the nameless yellow
flowers thriving in the useless logs,
or dots of light all night about the far end
of the lake, the dawn arrival of the idiot
with catfish—most of all, above the lake
the temple and our sanctuary there?

Nothing dies as slowly as a scene.
The dusty jukebox cracking through
the cackle of a beered-up crone—
wagered wine—sudden need to dance—
these remain in the black debris.
Although I know in time the lake will send
wind black enough to blow it all away.